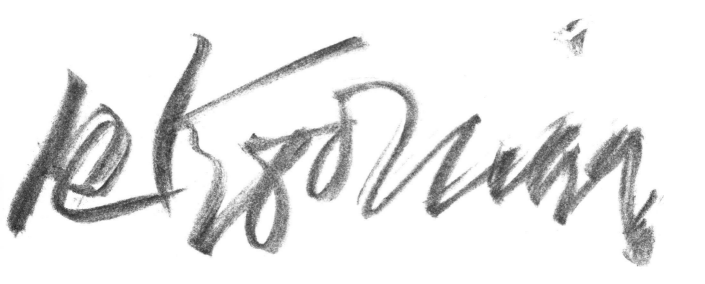

drawings

 Walker and Company, New York

Library of Congress Catalog Card Number: 67–30379
Published simultaneously in Canada by The Ryerson Press, Toronto
Printed in the United States of America

Published by Walker and Company, a division of Walker Publishing Company, Inc.,
in association with M. Knoedler & Co., Inc., New York

de Kooning

I am the source of a rumor concerning these drawings, and it is true that I made them with closed eyes.

Also, the pad I used was always held horizontally. The drawings often started by the feet . . . but more often by the center of the body, in the middle of the page.

There is nothing special about this, I admit, and I am certain that many artists have found similar ways . . . but I found that closing the eyes was very helpful to me.

Many drawings were made this way, and it was suggested to make this book.

I was very pleased with the idea and these 24 drawings were selected.

de Kooning

This volume reproduces, in exact size,
24 charcoal drawings executed by de Kooning in 1966.
Clarke & Way, Inc. and Crafton Graphic Company, Inc., New York,
have produced the book which was designed
by Julio Silva of Paris.